OUR SENSES

How Touch Works

Sally Morgan

PowerKiDS press.

New York

Published in 2011 by The Rosen Publishing Group Inc.
29 East 21st Street, New York, NY 10010

First Edition

Editor: Nicola Edwards
Designer: Robert Walster
Picture researcher: Shelley Noronha
Series consultant: Kate Ruttle
Design concept: Paul Cherrill

Library of Congress Cataloging-in-Publication Data

Morgan, Sally.
   How touch works / Sally Morgan. — 1st ed.
      p. cm. — (Our senses)
   Includes index.
   ISBN 978-1-61532-556-6 (library binding)
   ISBN 978-1-61532-565-8 (paperback)
   ISBN 978-1-61532-566-5 (6-pack)
   1. Touch—Juvenile literature. I. Title.
   QP451.M72 2011
   612.8'8—dc22

                              2009044493

5810

Photographs:
Cover Nicole S Young/istock; title page Patrick Oberem/istock;
p2 Rob Cruse/istock; p4 Bananastock/ Jupiter Images/ImagePick;
p5 Aldo Murillo/istock; p6 Katrina Brown/Shutterstock;
p7 Lindqvist/istock; p8 Martyn f. Chillmaid; p9 Stacy
Barnett/istock; p10 Nicole S Young/istock; p11 Peter
Cairns/Ecoscene; p12 Benjamin Howell/Shutterstock;
p13 © Tim Pannell/Corbis; p14 © Wolf/zefa/Corbis;
p15 © Ned Frisk/Corbis; p16 © Roy McMahon/Corbis;
p18 Patrick Oberem/istock; p19 Rob Cruse/istock;
© Todd Pusser/naturepl.com; p21 Michael Gore/Ecoscene;
p22 (both) Martyn f. Chillmaid; p23 Martyn f. Chillmaid

Manufactured in China
CPSIA Compliance Information: Batch #WAS0102PK: For Further Information
contact Rosen Publishing, New York, New York at 1-800-237-9932

Web Sites

Due to the changing nature of Internet
links, PowerKids Press has developed
an online list of Web sites related to
the subject of this book. This site is
updated regularly. Please use this link
to access this list:
http://www.powerkidslinks.com/os/touch

Contents

 Touch

Every day we touch many different things, such as the clothes that we wear and the food that we eat.

When we tie our shoelaces, we touch them with our fingers.

Touch is one of our five senses. We touch things to find out about our surroundings. Touch protects us, too.

Touching someone we love makes us feel happy.

Our five senses are sight, hearing, touch, smell, and taste.

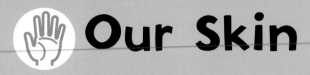

Our Skin

We touch using our skin, from our face to our fingertips to our toes. Hairs grow from the skin. These hairs help us to feel things, too.

We can feel with every part of the skin that covers our bodies.

Thick skin covers the soles of our feet. Thin skin covers our eyelids. The skin on our arms and legs is smooth but it is wrinkled on our elbows and knees.

Loose skin covers our knees so that we can bend our legs.

Touch and the Skin

When we touch something, special detectors in the skin send messages to the brain. The detectors can feel hot and cold, pressure and pain.

Blind people read Braille using their sense of touch.

Braille is a system of tiny raised dots that spell out words.

The skin on our fingertips, lips, and the back of our neck is very sensitive to touch. The thick soles of our feet feel very little.

Rashes make our skin feel itchy.

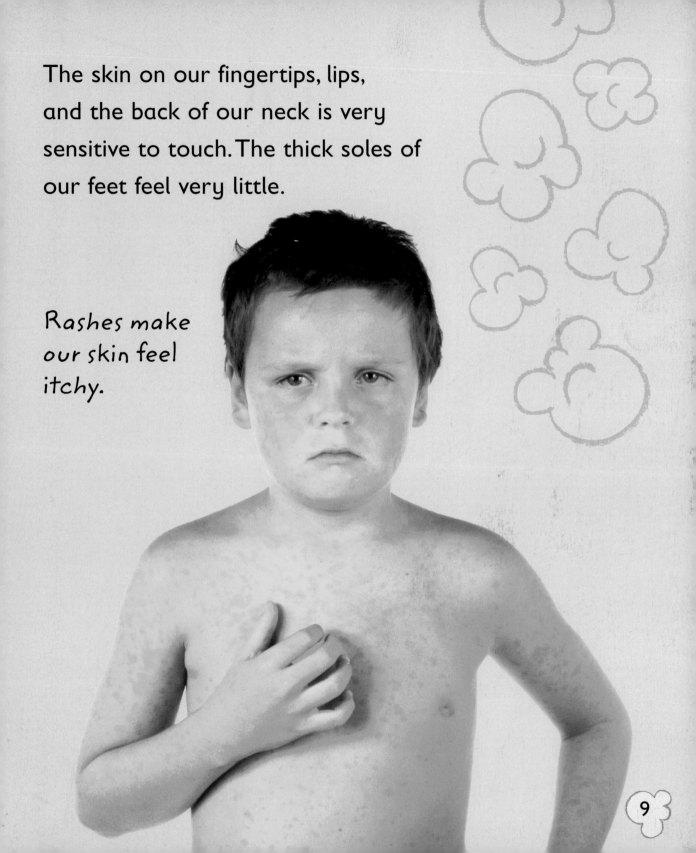

Textures

When you run your fingertips over the surface of an object, you feel its texture. Feel the cover of this book. It has a smooth, slippery surface.

Sand has a gritty and rough texture.

We use many different words to describe texture. Textures can be rough or smooth, bumpy or squashy, prickly or fluffy.

What textures would you feel if you were walking through this wood?

Can you think of any other words for textures?

Hot or Cold?

Our skin can feel if something is hot or cold. For example, a melting ice cube feels cold when we touch it. A towel straight out of the dryer feels warm.

Touching food with our lips and tongue tells us if it is hot or cold.

In cold weather, we cover our skin with warm clothes. In hot weather, we wear thin, light clothing so that our skin does not get too hot.

Our skin can tell the difference between a warm breeze and a cold wind.

Warning Touch

Our sense of touch helps to protect us from danger. When we touch a hot object, our skin feels the heat. We do not have to think about how to react. Instantly, we pull our finger away.

Ouch! Touching the sharp spines of a cactus can be painful.

These instant reactions are called reflexes. We cannot control a reflex. It happens without our brain being involved.

Kitchens can be dangerous places and our reflexes protect us from harm.

Protecting the Skin

Skin can be damaged by sunlight. Our skin burns if we stay in the sun for too long. Sunburned skin feels very painful. We can protect our skin by covering it with sunscreen.

If you are playing in the sun, use sunscreen to protect your skin.

Cold weather can harm our skin, especially the skin on our fingers and toes. In extreme cold, unprotected fingers and toes may freeze and feel numb.

In cold weather, we protect our skin by wearing thick gloves and shoes.

If our skin is harmed, our sense of touch works less well.

Using Touch

We use our sense of touch to find out information about our surroundings. Imagine walking barefoot along a path with your eyes closed. Your sense of touch would tell you if the ground was wet, bumpy, or slippery.

Babies use touch to explore their world.

We use touch when we pick up objects, hold a fork at mealtimes, and play musical instruments. Our fingers help us to play with toys and use a computer keyboard.

We use our sense of touch to plant seeds and seedlings, to pick fruit, and pull up vegetables.

Animals and Touch

Many animals use touch to locate food or to find their way around. Touch is very important to animals that have poor eyesight, such as moles and elephants.

The star-nosed mole has tentacles around its nose that it uses to touch.

Animals use their sense of touch when they look after their young. Some animals use their fingers to keep their fur clean. This is called grooming.

This monkey is picking off dirt and fleas from the fur of another monkey.

Glossary and Further Information

Braille writing made up of small, raised dots that blind people can read

brain the control center of the body, found inside the head

detectors structures in the skin that pick up signals, such as pain, pressure, heat, and cold

numb without feeling

pressure force pushing or pressing down on something, for example, pressing on a button

rashes itchy red patches of skin

reflex an instant reaction

sensitive able to detect or feel something

Books

Animals And Their Senses: Animal Touch
by Kirsten Hall
(Weekly Reader Early Learning Library, 2005)

The Sense of Touch
by Elaine Landau
(Children's Press, 2009)

World of Wonder: Touch
by James De Medeiros
(Weigl Publishers, 2009)

You Can't Taste Pickle With Your Ear
by Harriet Ziefert
(Blue Apple Books, 2006)

Index

MAY 2011